Foreword

I was very moved by Ann's p
beauty. Saint Francis saw all na
He would say, "My God and m
with love. He saw all nature as reflecting God's love.

> Be praised, my Lord, through all your creatures,
> especially through my lord Brother Sun,
> who brings the day; and you give light through him.
> And he is beautiful and radiant in all his splendour!
> Of you, Most High, he bears the likeness.
> Praised be You, my Lord, through Sister Moon the stars;
> in heaven you formed them clear and precious and beautiful.
> – Canticle

This expresses what I see in Ann's poetry. She also has deep reflections on the Cross in this work. In our world and culture we find that those who suffer are marginalised or rejected. Yet for St. Clare and St. Francis the Cross was the most visible expression of God's love for us. St. Bonaventure speaks of the Cross when he said:

> Christ on the Cross
> bows His head,
> waiting for you,
> that He may kiss you;
> He stretches out His arms,
> that He may embrace you;
> His hands are open,
> that He may enrich you;
> Hs body is spread out,
> that He may give
> Himself totally;
> His feet are nailed,
> that He may stay there;
> His side is open for you,
> that He may let you enter there.

Ann's writings are very much in this spirit.

She goes on to show how this will lead us to care for others. Love expresses itself in compassion for those who suffer. This moment is summed up by St. Clare: "Be strengthened in the holy service which you have undertaken out of a burning desire for the poor crucified, who for the sake of all of us took upon himself the passion of the cross."

Fr John O'Brien OFM

Acknowledgement:

This book is dedicated to all who have helped me on my spiritual journey which I would find impossible to separate from my life journey – all who have cheered me on as a runner in the race. Special words of gratitude go to Fr John O'Brien OFM and my brother John McKeever for their kindness and support in the production of this book.

Ballycastle Beach

On golden sand clean and wide
The children played for hours.
Later with crude, sharp-edged stones
They struck and hacked at
What they called the chipping rocks:
Two rugged, weathered basalt mounds,
One part-submerged, the other beached and steady.
And as they worked to gain new holds
Or sat on top while sizing up the bay
It seemed the world was easy for the taking,
All that could be conquered in one day.

Joy

Clad my soul in gladness Lord
So that the threads that bind heaven and earth
Will hold fast through every season of the heart
And that the workings of grace
Manifest in your peoples
Will be as canticles sung
As icons written
As beauty exalted.

The Power of God

God knows
The reason for
The twist of orange
Round the lace hole
Of the seabird's marble eye.
He numbers
The fine cloud lines
That make up
A mackerel sky.
In His all - knowingness,
No mysteries exist;
There is no question-
Omnipotence is His.

Northern Foreshore

Reclamation would not be easy here
Without a fight, the sea has clearly
Defined its hold, marking these walls
Noxious green that slimes onto
Thicknesses of resistance.
You moved south where warmer winds
Rounded the corners of your Ulsterisms,
Yet it is to this same spot you return
Time and time again, your painter's
Eye scanning the coastline, your mallow
Cheeks ever-resinous with rain.

Cushendun Beach

The hull of a white-sailed yacht
Is in line with the horizon
As a fisherman casts out
On an incoming tide.
A washed-up dog fish is turned backwards
And forwards by the motion of the water,
Its back slate-grey, its belly tide-white.
Gannets fly and dive, then swiftly
Regain height despite water-weighted wings.
Slender grasses sway in the sand dunes,
Behind is Rockport Lodge * – the poet's home in the Glens.
Looking now I wonder which her favourite window was,
Which light she wrote best by,
And of the little that has remained unaltered here,
What most caught her eye.

Home of Glens poet Moira O'Neill

Coast and Glen

It's a sanctifying moment
When the soul's immersed and cleansed
By the ribbon of bright water
As it courses through the Glens.
To discover above Red Bay
Where the high cross stands at Layde
How the sandstone work of masons
Bears sound witness to their trade.
To see stubble left by balers,
Or pink fuchsia in a hedge,
A rooster by a farmyard gate
Or a guillemot on a ledge,
Instinctively protective
Of the egg clutch in the nest
Is to drink the cup of nature
And know it's heaven-blessed.

Questions and Answers

He moves barefoot through grass and reeds
One hand's sweep can scythe a field,
Some have asked if what I hear,
If what I see
Is real or plain imaginary.
The answer lies somewhere in the rain
That strings glass beads
On wires and frames
And springs the earth to life again
That it might yield fine barley.

Nora B

On the evening before the ship sailed
She whispered a valediction
Into the ear of the wind -
Words not meant for the left behind,
And like a best friend
The wind blew westwards towards the sea
And scattered her words
Like bangles of roses on the waiting water.
Circles of cormorants and shags
Waked her leaving at first light
And watched us as we cried -
I and a Brent goose
With sand grains in its eyes.

The Cherry Trees

Always a source of disappointment,
How seemingly in an instant
The beautiful blossom is gone,
But the ground with its covering of
Pink snow
Consoles us for a time-
Though we have lived in pleasant
Shadows long enough
To know that off the tree
And after a night of rain
Each petal will shrivel and fade
And be lost to us again.

The Master

When Jesus sat talking with James and John
As night edged in over ebbing waters,
Did His words hang in the humid air
Like grapes on invisible vines,
To be plucked and shared,
Savoured in a time when finer dust
Would trickle from their sandals,
And the unfamiliar stir longings
For brotherhood, for signs,
For reminders of the sense of homeliness
That marked a Jesus-centred Galilean night.

Two or Three

Characteristic irregularity
Of floor–trailing feet is
My cue to watch and wait
While she side–steps
Into her favourite seat;
Then with an awkward
Movement of her head,
She turns towards me
Across the aisle
And smiles, then waves
And makes a face that says
'It's cold outside', as she
Blows make-shift heat
Into her bloodless hands.
This bond of ours
Commands few words,
The air is silent, deep.
Much is pondered in the heart
Of which the lips daren't speak.

Autumn Poem

Even when the last leaf
Is past its clinging on
And tree after tree in the forest
Sings a soulful, leafless song
The seedlings of the fruits of spring
Are dreams that are coming on
In the mulch of imagination
Round the mists of a watery dawn.

Until I Rest in Thee

Temper the wind, Lord,
Soften the ground where I lie
Let me sleep and dream
My head
Against your breast
Let me hear in the silence
Of the night the rhythmical beat
Of your heart
As I place my life
My body, my cares
In your keeping
Pray let me rest
Until the first piercing of light
Sends a rush of blood round
My cold bones
And stirs me enough
To know I have survived.

Reconciliation

A cascade of tamarisk sways in the easterly breeze,
A blackbird sings a song of praise before first light
A blazing star on the charcoal coat of night
Is guide for the sea-farer cast on a troubled tide
Absolution is a hand raised high
Drawing down that which the world cannot give
And there is peace in the soul.

Transformation – Lenten Poem

A forty day call to holiness
Through prayer to the Father
Through fasting in desert loneliness
And journeying far beyond the familiar
Until we reach that place,
An oasis, a garden of fruit
Round which pitched tent roofs are
Pierced by perfect truths
And the giver of life
Is revealed in shimmering stars.

Cherry Tree - North Belfast

The branches blossom-laden
Have, like children,
Climbed over the garden wall
Needing space
To stretch their limbs
Needing freedom to be themselves
No harm they say
Nobody's getting hurt
We're just seeing what's out here
We've waited long enough
To grow enough
To bloom where we're planted
We've waited long enough to take the whole world in -
In as much as Kansas Avenue is the world
On this bright April day.

The Window of His Eyes

He looks upon the world through the window of His eyes
We are more beautiful than stars to him
In our breathing out and in
There is the movement of a thousand wings
And in the silent language of the soul
Light plays with light in facets fit for kings.
We have the treasures of the world and more
If we but trim our lamps
And gaze on Him.

I am what I am in God

I am the tree.
When I am not the tree, I am the field.
When I am not the field I am the breeze
That weaves its way among the leaves.
I am the seed sown.
I am the mound and the hill.
I am the shoal that never sleeps
In a faraway sea where purple weeds are
Rooted in the deep.
I am what I am in God.

Earth Hour Poem

Earth is the song of songs
The grass at dawn dew-laden

Earth is clay and wattle
Ocean and wind
Fish in an opalescent bowl

Earth is tree and you and me
And the leaf and petal
Pattern of our dreams

Earth is herd and hill
And peaty river bends
And sheughs and ditches
Earth is grief and pull
And toss and loss

Earth is spin and peal
And ancient toll
Calling forth
The people to their God.

"LAUDATO SI', mi' Signore"

Between the wind and the seas
And the birds and the trees
There is music

Between the seeds and the showers
The grain and the flours
There is bread

Between the lines and the spaces
The day and the night
There is time

Between the labour and the rest
The prayer and the repose
There is love.
There is love.

Miracles of Grace

Often God's answers come
In subtle form
Imperceptible to the senses
Yet making manifest
The hidden works of his hand;
The divine plan
The master strokes
The shaping of His likeness
In our lives.

Poverty and Riches

I can cast a stone across water
And watch the ripples.
I can smile at a stranger
Along a mud road
And shower silent blessings.
I have the power to lift
A burden pressing
On another's shoulder.

I am poor in my brother's eyes
But like sands blowing over
In deserts of more
I hold treasures untold
To hand and in store

Curfew

There is no law to say we cannot sing
Among the splashing of plump raindrops.
There is no law inhibiting us from dancing on lush
grass,
Or leaning our backs against cropped hedgerows
To gaze at the stars.
But in some inner worlds
There is imposed upon the soul
A kind of curfew,
A voluntary forbiddance,
A refusal of the light.

Visitation

All I can recall now
Is an exchange between two
Whose presence to each other,
And to the room,
Exuded a kind of sweet-scented mystery.
A sense of invigoration
Like spring-fresh air blowing
Down a corridor
At the end of which
Sky, white as
The white of the eye,
Beckons the beholder to
Something promising beyond....

And in the end I went,
As people in dreams often do,
Silently,
Solemnly out into the new day.

Nativity of the Blessed Virgin Mary

It's a girl !
Joachim hurried home
His face bright with joy
All the neighbours gathering
Wishing him well
Evening sun reflected on water
Gathered in vessels
New fabrics ready
And Anne whose face was aglow
With newfound motherhood
Buried her head then somewhere between father and child
A threesome of
Wordless wonder.

Heaven and Earth

Mary, my Mother, you travelled over hillsides to be with your dear cousin Elizabeth. There was great excitement and joy, humility and wonder, on what was a unique occasion and joyful mystery. Let me be ever mindful especially in times of doubt and weakness, that when I receive your Son in the Eucharist, heaven visits earth, and I am wedded to sweet blessedness in a manner that transcends time and space.

Wheat

Today I will be the grain
That will fall to the ground
And be the cause of new growth.
A shoot will rise from darkness
Because of me.
If I die to myself
Day by day
In little things
New space will be freed up.
And God in his generosity
Will fill the vacuum
With His being.
Should vanity send me
In search of myself
Let me find nothing
Except what is lost in God.

Music

We lift up our hearts.
The buried song resounds
Once more.
From ocean depths
To highest heaven
There soars
In silence, and in singing,
The voice of man
And earth's mute praises ringing.

Tantum Ergo

'Tantum Ergo' is for me the hound of heaven. The first hearing of it that registered with me was when I was a young teen. There are many long blurry absences between then and now, but yet it has persistently followed me and although I know no Latin it speaks the language of love to me, and although I cannot sing, my heart sings every time I hear it. It seems like there is a deep attachment and connectedness there that does not diminish with time. Through the beauty of music I can know God's abiding love for me, His patience and endurance. What joy it is to be enthralled by airs of sacredness, touched by the divine.

A Calvary of Sorts

Some people die
Not on a cross as we know it
Not with nails and mockery all around
But yet they die
A hundred little deaths
In a daily trudge to somewhere and back
Their breathing laboured as they reach the brow of the hill

Some people die
On a Calvary of sorts
Near me
Close to you
They give to God
In a fashion all their own
The very thing He gave to them
With all the love they've known.

Sight

I did not see the wind
But I saw a rain drop
Blown clean off a leaf
That had been shaken

I did not see the secret place
Into which the rain drop fell
But I saw how the earth
Changed colour
Upon its passing

I was not there
When Jesus spoke to the crowds
Or when he made the blind man see
But the paste of clay and spittle
Brings life-giving hope to me.

Muintir na Mara

This shoreline is awash
With hidden industry.
The rotting timbers
Of a weather-bleached fishing boat
Are sudden shanty-towns
To the storm-cast creatures of the sea.

Odd habitats spring up
Under the weft of local weeds.
Their tangled tresses are
Combed, and then uncombed,
By the tide's careless caresses.

Sunset brings its own peculiar calm
To dunes and yellow-grey sands.
Gulls swoop low
And just as quickly rise
Flash-flooding with snowy under-wings
The violet-vaulted sky.

Trees

God knew what he was about when he made trees. He knew we would look to them and see models of ourselves, metaphors for our lives. Great pines growing side by side for generations speak of solidarity, strength in numbers. Or a hawthorn twisted by the punishing winds of time might depict resoluteness, standing one's ground, of being ourselves when the world rages against and around us. The beauty and dignity of trees can be compared to a wild lily unfolding for the first time in the growing brightness of the dawning air. Slowly its beauty is revealed; hesitancy gives way to eloquence and the world is blessed. So it is with trees. By cleansing the air for us they teach us how we can silently serve others. Their steadfastness teaches us to be calm in the storms of life. Wild nature's hand teaches us that we are never really in control. Sometimes we need to bend if we are not to break. We bend to the will of the Creator. We become alert to the promptings of the Spirit yet the centre core remains the same. Beauty and integrity lie within; we are God's through and through.

Judas

The night deposited its dust of gold
Upon His robes, upon His trembling shoulders.

Even the ancient olive trees looked to Him
Intent upon administering a balm.

And soon the angels came
With cups of comfort overflowing

The hour had come
On fast-approaching feet that brought the
Betrayer's lips to rest upon the pallid cheek.
The lamb was led away.

Later in a lonely field
Earth told its nature in a silvery heap

That lay beneath a body stilled
By twin-branched guilt and grief

Nature's Child

Fly high bright bird
Let nothing but light
Penetrate the dark membrane of your wings.
Carve for yourself a meteoric path
That hails the dawn that greets you.
Then rest a while
In waysides of the wild;
You and holy nature like
Mother and child.

I shall lift my eyes to the hills (Psalm 120)

No more trailing of feet
No more downcast looks.
I shall lift my eyes to the hills
And there I shall see his works
Spilling down from balconies of dawn.

Joyful fountains pour a morning psalm
Form a crown of glory
Saffron and green
Amethyst and blue
Filling the light of my eyes.

Graves

Thread-like inscriptions
On sunken slanted stones
Are all that remain.
Tributes to mothers, friends, brothers
And farmers, midwives and merchants…

Chisel-cut births and deaths
Witness to the care of kith and kin and the
Neighbourly dues of old.

Love

From love that
Endures all
The holy breath of heaven
Prays us into being.

Love lavishes upon us
All that is good.
Love beckons us to the fire of His heart
Where we can be consoled.
Against the biting winds of trial
We find strength
And raise ourselves by faith
To higher planes.

The Hills

Today I feel drawn to the hills,
To chapels without walls
Where I shall meet
With nature and my maker.
Each rock, each clump of heather
Speaks of beauty, of endurance,
Of season and of change.
Along the clay banks of a trickling stream
Music fit for matins is made.
Amid these reaches of unworldliness
There is pure celebration.

Come, Holy Spirit

Come, Holy Spirit
Set the world ablaze
That all might know you
That perfect peace might reign.

May every heart desire
Above all worldly gain
The coming of your power
In tongues of burning flame.

Fire of God

Still the Spirit comes
With purifying fire
With power of wind that blows the slender reeds
And stirs and wakes the slumbering seeds.

In hearts laid bare his light will shine
And to the world reveal
Mercy's fruits from holy hands
Marked at birth with chrism's seal.

Still the Spirit comes
As fire, as oil, as dove, as breeze
But most of all as breath of Love
That fans to flame the fire of God.

Nothing but the skies

When storms rage
Let me retreat into the chasm of Your heart.
Such peace, such soul-relief!

I shall immerse myself
Again and again
In the mystery-waters of mercy.
Renewed again I will rise
Like a flower head lifted to the light
By nothing but the skies.

Ecology

Gale-whipped trees splay the wagging fingers
Of old women in snagged shawls and
Waves in tumult spew like the foaming mouths
Of ancestors who cannot stop themselves
From writhing and crying out;
Accountability stares us in the face.

All nature rages against such mindless greed
That stifles nations
Turning beauty on its head
Uprooting the living
And desecrating the dead.

Wings

When we see the light of joy in a face
When we see eyes dance
We learn that there is more to life
Than brokenness.

We learn that poverty too
Has angel wings.
The spirit within
Is not imprisoned
By a ribbed cage
But has passage of its own.
We soar in the sheer joy
Of being a child of God
And born to sing.

Go Forth and Tell

It is a sign of God's presence among us that souls gathered in prayer experience tangible joy. They experience something of the divine nature. Tears may be turned into dancing. Burdens brought to the foot of the cross seem lighter and less cumbersome. Humility can weave the most wonderful thread among souls, picking up on one person's pain, and on another's anxiety and so on until we are all part of the one fabric which God adorns with light and hope. Prayer is invisible to the eye but fortifying to the heart, flooding its recesses with peace the world cannot give. We taste of it and it tastes good. Not content then with keeping it to ourselves, we are compelled to go forth and tell.

For where two or three have gathered together in my name, I am there in their midst.
Matthew 18:20

Nativity

As a journey is made long by lateness
The waiting proves intense.
Now, at last, the hour arrives when
Peace and beauty reconcile.
Bethlehem loses nothing to the fall of night
Illumined from on high, by heaven's lasting light.

Noise of the world

Lord, release me from
The noise of the world,
The clatter of things.
Entanglements
In my head and in my life
Roll in like waves
To batter and seize the silent shores.

Lord, let me hover
In that space between
Heaven and earth.
Allow me sufficient grace
To return to the here and now
To embrace with open arms
All that becomes beautiful and
Bearable in You.

Presence

There are no words
Neither a coming nor going.
Silence itself communicates a
Power greater than
We can know.

By listening we place ourselves
At the door of
The house of prayer;
Expecting we know not what
But knowing real presence there.

Rose Garden

Every rose is an emblem of love,
A composition of colour and scent.
The stemmed flower triumphs
Over the thorns twisted and bent.
The knot of a bud
Tenderly coaxed
Reveals and releases
To the world a room
Where beauty hangs on every wall;
Yet shies at the eye of the moon.

But come the morning, come the light
True joy is told;
Rose after flowered rose assembles
Vibrant, majestic and bold.

Beyond the gate

In early morning quiet
It is almost possible to believe
That I am earth's sole inhabitant
Drinking in this lush light
Under dappled leaves.

Perched on a low-leaning branch
Surveying a landscape
Buttered with Irish light
These times are laced with promise.

All that can be seen
All that captivates and
Makes the heart sing
Is but a fingerprint
Of the maker
Beyond the gate.

Desert

What did Jesus see in the
Silken skies above the desert
When night came
Like a steel blade
That pressed a cold sweat
Upon his flesh?

What did he strain to hear
When the homely echo of
Family was distanced
By empty desert acres?

What did he pray for in his heart
But the strength to bear
By the bones of his humanity
All that would be placed there.

What did he hunger for
But unity and peace in
The bread of his own body;
The famine and the feast.

The Great Call

He came to me out of the shadows
Like a sun shaft
Through a canopy of leaves
And I knew in my deepest being
That Love's sharp-edged sweetness had pierced my soul.
I had heard my name borne on the breath of the wind,
And knew that the breath of the wind was Him, my God, my all.

For a friend who has passed on

All that weighed you down is lifted now
Light upon the April air
Scribbled lyrics in old notebooks rise
Like spiral stairways to the vaulted skies.
God rest you friend
And may new life begin
Enfolded in such tenderness
That is only found in Him.

Purpose

Sometimes I forget
That the firmament and the waters
Come from His hands.
I fail to remember
That all that has been given us
Has come from a beautiful thinker;
That all that is created
Has been worked in some way through the
Golden veins of His being.

In all these years
Of moving, walking, thinking
I am as much a part of His creation
As anything or anyone
Loved in such a special way
That I am centred in His heart.
What happens matters
Not only to me
Not only to the world about me
But to God.

Let my purpose then be attuned to His will
Let my step be one with His
Let me lose myself and take on the nature
Of the one who is known as Love.
Let come the One who sows seeds
So that the tree can take on leaf and leaf and leaf
While all the while singing in the roots of its being;
Let that be my life's work too
Let me become a living work of praise.

Grace

Cleaved by grace
Your heart split open
Issuing forth all the love
A heart can hold at any given time
And like pure gold
Its brightness was a lamp for hungry eyes
In search of brightness
In search of proof that goodness and God
And grace are so intertwined
So as to be one in ways
That causes the mind to dwell on things
Like the poetry of night skies
For this too, like your heart,
Is bountiful until the dawn
And even then, though hidden from our eyes,
Spawns brightness on and on.

Gaudete Garden

The 'o' at the centre of joy
Is the unseen-to-the eye shape
Of a blackbird's throat
As from its orange bill
Spills note upon note
That makes of a modest garden
A timbered stage that hosts
Such singing, such showmanship,
Such undiluted praise.

Advent Poem

Bless my soul, Lord,
At this time of waiting
And anticipation.

May your word be as benediction
As I prepare the way for
The sovereign child
The Prince of Peace
Whose throne is clay
Whose realm is
The tabernacle of
The human heart
That bids Him stay.

Bless my soul, Lord,
At this time of waiting
For the promised one.
Let my creation be
A dwelling place fit for a king -
The Son of God most high
Who comes as light, as joy,
As flame-setter within.

Dream for the Children of Light

God has the answers before we pose the questions
His orchards are fragrant with fruits from seeds not yet planted
Paths are laid down for us before we can walk
Such is His love, His intention, His dream for the children of light.

Arranging the Flowers

The softest of prayers were shared
As flower heads passed through hands like beads,
They counted out the Aves
One till ten,
Then smiling, placing and replacing
They began again and kept on going
Until each vase was filled
The air around stilled
But for the sound of their own breathing
Amid the vases, floating, teeming.

Cavehill, Belfast

Sometimes we realise just how fortunate we are
When through a windy gap, between tall terraces,
We catch sight of Cavehill
Clothed in sage and gold.

Much like a celebrated seanchai
The hill has its own stories
That go back and back
To the very bones of time
When nothing was written down
But that which nature scribed in basalt lines.

Glenariff Waterfall

To the right, high above our heads,
From glistening outcrops
Of rock and red earth,
Side by side with ferny foliage,
Steady trickles of water, thin as harp strings
Seeped into the ground below.
And to the left a torrent, which as it thundered
To new depths, downpoured unstoppable,
Elemental, white scattering light.

Ardglass Harbour

One old fishing boat rests
Against a tide-marked wall,
Its timbers skinned
Warped and water-whitened,
The wheel-house gutted.
Suddenly, alarming cries pierce the air
As a fishing boat comes in,
Bulging nets of herring are
Lowered into crates,
Ice like milky quartz is shovelled on top.
Glazed dead eyes
Reflect the bird-whitened sky.
In the harbour now two seals,
Then one, then nothing but bubbles
Bursting on bright water.

Dolphins

Somewhere seaward of Magheramorne and
Glenarm
I spotted three dolphins at play.
Firstly they aired their noses in the salty air
Then their whole bodies
Appeared as dark rainbows that signal no gloom.

Rather, these sudden strokes of mastery
Fleeting, floating, lithe and bright
Showed forth sheer wildness
Brought forth delight.

City Sunset

The sun is slipping down behind Black Mountain
St. Peter's spires are lost to me till dawn
But in my head the pictures make a fountain
Of watercolours in tall, cascading form.
My mind reflects on suns in other cities,
A circumstance that finds us near or far,
Belfast or Beijing, our hearts are governed
By the who-ness of the persons that we are,
The knowledge of a light beyond the star.

Water

Water is gold
Gold that wets a dry mouth
Gold that irrigates the arid lands
Water is the gold of crocuses in bloom
Water is the rain that drums upon the roof
And causes bubbles
To flower in puddles
Water is gold
That earns its place
On the podium
In life's race
Water waves
And winds and wends
Water works
And earth sings
As splendour rises
Borne on heraldic wings.

Gazes

Lovingly You gaze on me, Lord.
I know it.
And through trial more than any other means
I have learned to gaze a little too -
Like when I look at the veined pattern
On a leaf
As it answers me back
With its beautiful green stare
When I ask about life,
About God,
About our being here.

Home

It's said in these parts
That the tall grasses are the nearest living relatives
To the old uncle of a hawthorn tree they call
Methuselah
And the earth underground
That has caked itself
Round the roots
Is family too.

What else can we cling to
Except that which we bed down in?
And when something larger than life trundles past
It is consoling to know
That there are hidden structures
Keeping us where we are
Providing the stability
We come to know as home.

Loughareema – The Vanishing Lake

Nobody heard the lake filling up
The watchman did not come
And yet it happened
The sky's beauty
Is now captured there
In the stillness you can hear God speak
His is an exquisite tongue
That sends souls cartwheeling
In delight that the earth
Has such things as vanishing lakes
Such times as our time
Such days as today.

Going Places

Bedraggled
Unwashed untended
Toe-peeping shoes past needing mended
Clothed in a carnival coloured shawl and wrap-
round swatches
Hair hidden but for a few strands framing a face
That tells its own beleaguered story
Deep-set eyes functioning, but only.
Not like the sparkling eyes
Of her younger dreaming self
Lithe body leaning over a bridge
That straddled peat-brown water
Where fallen leaves
Like ducks in a line were carried downstream -
Day of village pride
Of well-wishers gathering at the quayside
She'll go places, they said
Wait till you see!

Dawn Chorus

At break of day
God and wind together
Bear down on voice and feather.
The ground appears as if to float
On seas made buoyant
By throaty notes and trills
That warble their way downwards
Upwards, wherever wind wills
Leaving in their wake
Like carefree revellers
Joy for joy's sake.

Mercy is a River

Mercy is a river
That sows itself
In splashes
Providing water
For the thirsty
Who are terrified of the deep
And soul-sick for want
Of feeling wanted.

Lourdes – A Personal Reflection

When I think of Our Lady of Lourdes I think more of joy than sorrow, more of promise than dread. In some cases a pilgrimage to Lourdes is the first thing a person might consider when faced with illness and in other cases it might be the last when all other avenues have been tried. And yet many pilgrims leave with the same illness they came with, but they will quickly tell you they feel the better for having come. Is it the water that brings about the change? Is it the candlelight procession? Is it the communion of the sick - so many suffering people in one place, carers at every corner, ministers with blessed oils laying hands on heads and hands? Is it the atmosphere in the underground basilica, the incense and the Ave's? It would be impossible to put a finger on it. But whatever happens I would go so far as to say that Our Lady herself has a hand in it all, she moves to heal and comfort, she gazes with eyes of mercy, she touches hearts and souls. And that is miracle enough for most, miracle to ponder, to take home and talk about, miracle that brings joy into places of suffering, light into dark recesses of hearts and minds.

Setting Out

The old church building is gone and a new one is in its place
There are echoes of footsteps, of once familiar paths traced,
Whisperings of prayer,
Memories of christening robes and weather-beaten faces,
And the swaying of rosary beads in praying hands
All telling me that in a world of confessed and unconfessed wrongs
There are always right beginnings.

Answering

Answering can take a life time. Answering God, answering the questions we put to ourselves about life. Distraction, doubt, disinterest and even dismay are just some of the walls we come up against. But if we reach a bit of high ground or a windy gap we see more clearly the signs and markings that are there all the time, and we regain a sense of who we are - the person we have become since finding that answering brings us closer every time – closer to understanding, closer to finding what we're looking for.

Space for God

There's a kind of moving out that takes place on the inside. Space gets freed up, rubbish gets dumped, and before you know it there's a Guest room. And when we see what the Guest can do in one small room we set about clearing more space for Him for what we had before was emptiness while in Him is fullness beyond compare.

In the White of the Fire

Greening the pastures, with nothing but the glance of an eye
Setting in place all that is under the sky
How great is our God! Amazing in all His ways
Painterly, masterly, potter of earthen-bright clays.
Tempering winds with a simple command of his hand
Banishing ills, smoothing to flatness the sands
Raising our minds to heights where only holiness dwells
God of all goodness, Lord of the dip and the swell.

Sower of seed, maker of stars of night
Will of the Father, Love of the Spirit of light
Fashion our hearts so as to burn with desire
To be moulded to likeness of Him in the white of the fire.

Love can make it happen

With no shoes love can move around,
With no words love can attract attention,
With little acts of subterfuge, love can give and give again
And miss nothing, and lack nothing,
With no shoes love can move around
With no words love can make it happen.

Willow

In the shade of a willow with its inbuilt grace
We sat and chatted
Round a table of dappled light
Socially distanced but engaged
In each other's catch-up time
Not measured by clock hands
But by coffees consumed
Laughs, shared memories,
The very best of good times.

Tollymore Forest

Standing under a Cedar of Lebanon
Was a prayerful experience
For I could not but think of God
Near the restful waters of the Shimna
With the backdrop of the Mournes;
And for a while at the Hermitage
There was no denying
The supernatural calm
Amid an all-round leafy loveliness,
Chapel-ed with tree-top psalms.

Divis Mountain

Something of God was revealed in
Lark song at invisible height
A first for me;
It was a thrilling gift of the air
As clear and sweet as could be dreamt of
On a Belfast hillside.

Easter Morning, Knocknacarry

High above in branches limed with light
A blackbird sings on my behalf -
Something from the Book of Psalms
For the risen Christ, something
To delight the angels.
What is glory but man at his best?
The hunger I feel inside,
Just now, is put to rest.
In peaceful ways God hears my need
And through the songs of birds
He fills my soul with grace
And I am healed.
To speak with Him on mornings
Such as these is a window
Onto heaven through high trees.

Oh sing, blackbird, sing!
Fill these glens with music
And sweet praise
For Jesus Christ is risen
And darkness, like the stone,
Is rolled away.

Derelict House in the Glens

Behind the roadside house
Lilac blossoms overhang the rocky burn,
Ivy branches imitate art form
In a contrivance of twists and turns.
Sedges, hawkweeds and nettles stand
Well past shoulder height,
Where grave-faced boards hide windows
Stone walls are a silver-trailed white.
In an air that is sweetened with heat
Blue and orange glow bright
As smoke drifts up from the chimney
And surrenders itself to the night,
Grouped voices of chattering children
Can be heard at the rise of the latch
As the door of the cottage opens
And the hands on the clock turn back.

Rathlin Island

Westwards, past the harbour, buzzards soar silently
Above hills of abounding heather.
Beyond the meadowsweet of marshland
And mallard of fresh water,
We reach, by rough road, the Bull Light.
Castellated sea stacks are nesting sites
For fulmars and kittiwakes,
Whose incessant soulful cries
Drown out the wash below.
An endless rancid rise of fish oils
Invades the nostrils,
While eyes and mind take in
The bastion that is the West Light,
Built with fearlessness and skills honed against
The hacking chillness of a might
That floored a thousand wrecks,
And hoarded bone on bone.
These islanders knew suffering:
The repeated bloodlust of invaders,
A people slaughtered almost to a man.
From Cnoc na Scridlin, on stormy nights
A relentless sound of wailing
Is carried downhill by the wind
Lest the living should forget
An ancestry thinned to a bloodline
A heritage enshrined in island pride.

Patrick on Slemish Mountain

I gazed up at the sky and saw a field:
Stars scattered like seed on darkest soil,
And where the moon advanced no cloud concealed
A watchful eye above a world of toil,
While later, through the thinning dark converged
Ascending notes of dawn-addressing birds.

Remembrance

Summer remnants do not warm us now
When the first winds bite
And though her dark colours try to gleam,
November's is a sombre kind of light.
A wreath of poppies ignites upon a bier
Or glistens on some newly-opened earth
While an Ave is chanted round a cross.

All nature listens,
Remembering the dead
Their lives
Their sacrifice
Our loss.

According to his purpose

According to his purpose I am here
A path I did not choose made out for me.

Each petal on the rose
Each branch on the living tree
Comes under the gaze
Of the loving God;
That is as light to me.

According to his purpose I am here
What gift and joy it is!
This life, so dear.

And we know that in all things God works for the good of those who love him, who have been called according to his purpose. *Romans 8:28*

Rosary Musings in May

When I carry my beads on my person may I be reminded
Of the One who carried a cross for me.
When they sparkle as they catch the light of the sun
May I be mindful of Christ as light of the world.
When they're hidden from sight
May I understand that many things in life
Are hidden from our understanding
But we trust in God all the same the One
Whose power and presence and all-knowingness
Sustains us by the hour – the One
Who signals to us at first light
That a new day is beginning
And heeds our every whispered prayer -
All our Aves like incense rising
To the throne of grace.
All our Amens harmonising
As songs and choruses
Of gratitude and praise.

Mary of the Kind Eyes

Mary of the kind eyes
Look to us always with motherly love.
Mary of the hardships
Be one with us in times of trial.
Lady of the smile
Heal us and encourage us.

Queen of the Rosary
Lead us through the mysteries of our own lives.

Lady of Sorrows
Ease our suffering
That we might live in peace.

Mary of graces
Pour onto us this day
All we need to sustain us.

Spouse of the Spirit
Hear our prayers
All the days of our life.
Amen.

The Cross

Go to the Cross

If someone should spit in your face, hold back, walk away, and go to the Cross.

If someone by their words places you on a pedestal, be kind, say little, and go to the Cross, where words are washed away in water and blood.

If your heart and mind and body should ache to the point of weariness, go to the Cross even if you have to drag yourself step by step.

If someone should tell you are not good enough, go to the Cross, for there you will find One who dreamed of you before you were born, and deemed you worth dying for.

If you are burdened by past sin, go to the Cross and rest there at the nailed feet of the Saviour.

If the suffering of others grieves your spirit, go to the Cross.

If you can see no hope beyond the hour you find yourself in, go to the Cross and spend time with the One who knows the pain of isolation.

If you want to visit a friend or find one, go to the Cross.

If you miss someone carry them in your heart to the Cross.
When all is going well go to the Cross in thanksgiving.

If someone you love needs help go to the Cross first and work out from there the best thing to do.

If you feel the Cross is calling you.....respond.

If it is true that there is power in the blood of the Son who died for us,

If it is true that God gave us His only Son to free us from death – and we know this to be true

Then you and I can confidently go to the Cross over and over

Bringing with us

Those who stand at crossroads and corners

And who do not know the way.

Beauty and the Cross

Perhaps when you hear the bell ring out across the valley you will think about what it is to pray. Where will you find beauty this day? Maybe you will see it in the face of a friend, or in the bright eyes of a child, or a fragrance or hue will remind you of summer flowers in lush meadows. You may be humbled by the beauty of the artwork on a prison cell wall, or in the lean and lined face of an old person whose once labour-coarsened hands are now soft as a baby's.

Maybe you will hear beauty speak to your soul through strains of music or the sounds of the sea; or you will encounter it in the very depths of suffering when visiting someone you know whose life is wound round the wood of the Cross. The truth is beauty is never far away; it surrounds us and is within. Thus we who are made in the image and likeness of the loving God have much to celebrate amidst our pain, and much to sing about amidst our suffering. God and beauty are inseparable. God is in the beautiful, and we are in God. We trust and place our hope in Him who supports and sustains us.

Good Friday

An impassioned mist enveloped those
Who stood beneath the Cross

No ordinary man was this -
A veil of mourning covered the sun,
The temple curtain was torn from top to base,
The cold earth quaked as
All were plunged into an ecliptic night
When even the wood of Calvary stood
Bereft of heaven's light.

Exaltation of the Cross

The listening tree
Sings out the
Wedding vows
Of flesh betrothed to wood,
Of glory and all godly good.

As redemption stakes its claim
In rubric and in loss
Mankind too is lifted high
With Christ upon the Cross.

Accomplished

The wind's fingers
Strum against the stringed flesh of His shoulder wound
Producing a bittersweet dirge
Hauntingly out of tune

Last words heavy with sighs
Pierce the hearts of listeners

An upwards thrust
Of a lance
Brings forth water and blood
From the chalice
That is His body's sacred side -
Twin rivers reclaim space in daytime darkness
Sisters of salvation and mercy
Untrammelled and unafraid
Pour out a message for all mankind.

Nailed to the Wood

(1)
The broken body of the crucified Christ
Speaks silently to the broken world.
A famished child, strapped to a bent back,
Is again the sacred flesh
Nailed to the wood of the cross.

(2)
A dried-up riverbed
Comes to life again
And writes its own sweet music
On staves of sticks and cleft stones.
The flowering of the masses
Is the surge of goodness
That levers the tomb's round stone.

Followers of the Way

We do not descend when we embrace the cross. We may taste the salt of our tears, we may stumble under the weight of its burden, and we may bleed as the rough wood bruises and blisters our skin, but always, we are raised up. We ascend to the plain where Love dwells and breathes holy fire upon the world; to the height from which Our Saviour gazed upon His mother and His friend; to the level at which all is changed through, with and in Him. We rise above the confines of ourselves with all our weakness, sin and frailty, straight into the open arms of the loving God. We take up our cross and follow Him.

Scarlet Blooms

To be immersed in His wounds
Is to be in a sanctuary where scarlet blooms hang on walls,
And rivers, whole rivers, gush mercy.

Healing

Lord let me be as healer
To the suffering stranger.
May enough pass between us
In silence
For him to know
I would lend an ear and listen
Should he feel the urge
To open to the world
His hidden wounds.

Sorrowful Mysteries

The Agony in the garden
Lord, come to the assistance of those who are in agony, in body, mind or spirit. Send your angels to console them, and may You be present in those who comfort them. Help those who are suffering to unite themselves with You for the sake of the salvation of souls.

The Scourging at the pillar
Lord, forgive me for all the times I have scourged others by what I have said or done, or neglected to do. Forgive me for the lashings of my tongue, the slight and anger in my eyes, and the weight of my hand.

The Crowning with thorns
Forgive Lord my mocking ways, forgive those actions of mine that have burdened or belittled others. Let all your children live with the dignity that is their birth-right as Your sons and daughters, especially the homeless and dispossessed.

The Carrying of the Cross
Lord, let me take up my cross in imitation of You. When I fall, let me not abandon it by the roadside but instead accept offers of help from others so that I may persevere to the last.

The Crucifixion and death of Our Lord
Lord, it is only through dying to ourselves that we can become wholly alive in You. Mary, assist me, Jesus, be my strength in facing my mortality. Holy Spirit, be my light and guide, my wisdom and my friend

The Whole Picture

We leave the judging of others in the everyday to God because our sight is limited as is our knowledge. There is always another side. Whether it's a relationship or a character being talked about we cannot know the whole picture. The side a mother knows, the side a friend from schooldays knows, the side a neighbour saw on that day when she was in dire need. But most of all we cannot see what God sees through merciful eyes that take in the whole picture – the same eyes that have gazed on us, the same heart that knows us better than we know ourselves. To know a person through and through is to know them as only God knows them. May we come to know Him more.

Within The Wounds

Somewhere within the wounds
There is a language deeper than words
Deeper than wells
Deeper than woods

Somewhere within the wounds
There is the fragrance
Of love, of gift,
A heart of sacredness
An altar of the lamb

Somewhere within the wounds
Is where Christ is
And where I,
In my unworthiness,
Am
Somewhere within the wounds
Petals unfurl
As the flower of His sacred passion
Is loosed onto the world.

Hail, O Cross, Our Only Hope

There really is only one choice to be made in life – either we embrace the cross or we rail against it. All other choices, all other areas of life are affected and permeated by this first and most important choice. Whether we like it or not, the cross is part of our lives - run away and it will follow, try to exchange it for another and find you're worse off than before, but embrace it and you'll enter into a peacefulness that will bring meaning to your life, labour and love – such is this saintly embrace.

The cross can become for you a powerful symbol of hope. It can be an assurance - the only true one - that bridges the gap between this life and the next. We can look at the cross and say – 'here is my brother, Lord Jesus, who died that I might live, who rose from the dead so as to do away with death, who ascended to heaven to show me the way.'

A beautiful story is written in the wounds of the Saviour, such a heart-rending tale is there for the telling – over and over and over again. Embrace the cross, do not be afraid – it will be the making of you. Stand at the cross as did the faithful two – be one with them in a world of the misunderstood.

Tree of Mercy

Mercy is a tree whose roots formed on Calvary but now stretch across the world,
whose worth is told in countless different tongues that praise from earth to highest heaven, the Master, the one of the pierced side who by water and blood saves the sinner from himself and draws all men to God.

And He showed them His hands and His feet.
Luke 24:20

The hands of Jesus are holy and healing. Many a time they were immersed in salt water, and many a time splinters would have worked their way in under sensitive skin. Firstly they were the hands of a child, of a carpenter's helper, and later hands of a miracle worker.

But it is when we picture them in the red-rawness of vulnerability, with nail holes pierced through that the reality sinks in. All the pain of Calvary, all the agony in the garden, all the mockery and vileness, is summed up in two resurrected hands forever open, forever stretched out, forever giving of all that can be given by the sacred and selfless one who won for us a place at the heavenly table, a life beyond this life, beyond death – one that promises eternal glory to the followers of the way. We can stake our life on it - and all because of Jesus's laying down His own life for us - for you and me. Think mercy, and think tree, think wounds and think healing, think gift and think gratitude, think praise and think song that goes on and on....

Good Friday (2)

There are no words for that moment
When the temple veil was rent
As darkness overtook the hours
Or when water and blood streamed
To form a pool that seeped
Into the fleshy veins beneath
His wounded side.
There are no words for scenes
Like these
Yet there is a prayer
Constant in its inexpressible grief.
A cry on lips that reaches heaven
A breaking of the heart
That bruises nature
And shrouds the world.

Crucifix

The crucifix teaches while the learned sleep.
Beauty and eloquence seep into
The iconic depths of our being.
It is a sombre song wrung
From the body forlorn
A ringing in the ears
A wringing of the hands.

The final embrace
Of Mother,
Brother, lover -
Rings out in silent call
To all of the human race.

Truest Vision

No matter how hard people try, no matter how skilled they have become at concealment, the hurt they carry within has a way of slipping out from the shadows into the light even if only for a moment. A veil is lifted, the door to a secret garden blows open in a gust of wind, and in the ensuing moments before things are restored to normal, we glimpse the rugged cross, as real as if we were to reach out and touch it with our bare hands, and it takes our breath away. At such times we come to understand what a privilege it is to walk the royal road, to know that Christ is as near to us as we invite/ permit Him to be, and the truest and closest vision of our wounded neighbour is at the same time the truest vision of the suffering Christ that we in the world will ever see.

Taunting Voices

Jesus was taunted when on the Cross. "If you really are the Messiah then save yourself!" The real proof of who He is was in His staying on the cross for our sake rather than in His coming down. In the modern world there are many taunting voices calling on others to act like God, to assume Divine authority. But it was the will of the Father that was obeyed on the Hill of Calvary and no other. The only true peace that man can know is in submission of heart and mind and will to the all-powerful, all-wise and all-knowing God.

Healing Body of Christ

It is not with glue that God re-sets the broken fragments of our lives but with Himself. He enters into our brokenness just as He entered into abject poverty upon a wooden cross. In this world there are many places and occasions when we hang as He did upon a cross and in our acceptance of it we are humbling our unruly hearts and wills and giving our very lives over to the will of God. The mother of the sick child is at her station and although her body is drained of energy she knows she will not sleep until her child is well. She does everything possible to ease the child's distress and is a source of comfort to the baby. At the first sign of improvement all tiredness leaves the mother's body and she knows at that moment she could dance round the room with sheer joy at the sight of her own flesh and blood regaining colour and strength. Our sins impoverish us but God died to take our sins away. In spiritual as well as physical poverty we might well thirst for water and it is then that we, like the man in the bible story who sat for so long at the side of the pool, can slowly ease ourselves like he did into the healing body of Christ.

Suffering – Mary and us

The question is barely formed on our lips when the answer is already waiting in God. When we believe there is purpose for all created things we can know that there is meaning behind all suffering. While we don't have the answers, we do have God present to us and in us – Emmanuel, Emmanuel. The suffering in which Christ dwells causes us to act in practical and prayerful ways and in so doing we stand as Mary stood at the foot of the Cross. Hers was a silent station, dignified and composed, and that is the way for us. We watch, we wait and in utter powerlessness we trust to God all we cannot understand, sure in the hope that He will turn all things to the good, ridding the world of evil and suffering and drawing all men to himself.

Before an Icon

There is sadness in Mary's face
She knows the child she holds will suffer.
Thus she bids us all the more
To come to Him
To look to His wise eyes
That look to us.

She knows she holds the Son of God.
Knows too, like any mother
The painful price that she must pay
As sacrifice for others.

Be it done unto me was her prayerful response.
It afforded us such grace

That every hour in every time
Is changed by Mary's *fiat.*

Be it done unto me is our prayer too,
In humble imitation
Of one whose heart, though pierced and sore,
Bowed not to tribulation.

The God Within

Quite often we have pain that others cannot see. God himself can heal us with the balm of His own body. He comes to us in our deepest need and carries us to ease the load we feel upon our shoulders. It is nothing short of wondrous that each of us is loved in this way. It far exceeds any human love. We have within us the answer to unspoken prayers, the balm for wounds, and healing unction. We have within us the miracle of the Eucharistic Lord - through Him we flourish and in Him we have the promise of eternal life.

Sigh

So much passes between us without words. In the silence of the church sometimes we might hear an irrepressible sigh and we know immediately that God hears it too. Private prayer and wordless exasperation fly to God just as swiftly as the spoken word. The Spirit of consolation is near at hand. The ear of God is forever open to our cares. It was out of great love that He created us and back to that great love we are drawn day and daily, feast or famine, rain or drought.

Lord of all

I thirst for the lost ones,
For the waters of their hurt
To wash over the wounds of my sorrow.

I thirst for the wanderer,
Cup carelessly held in hand.
I thirst and all that is in me
Thirsts for every man.

Like a dry riverbed
Yearning for light kisses
From passing rain
I thirst for those who thirst
I am one with those in pain.

Words

We are moved when Christ's words on the cross speak to us today. Just as a sponge soaked in vinegar was no salve to the cracked lips of destitution and pain, mere litanies of pity do not ease the suffering of the children of God.

Temple

I cannot expect to be shielded from storms. I cannot seek a place away from trial. I dare not think that I shall never suffer; but I can know as sure as God is God, that I will be provided for as if I were His only child. I will be nourished and blessed; I will be given all I need to conquer sin, to fight my corner, to live the life God has willed for me. At Mary's hands there is a store of grace, the Sacred Heart of her son is brimming over with love and mercy, and the Eucharist is the source and summit of Christian life. These means of strength and sustenance are my temple's fortification. By the Spirit I am healed. In the Spirit I am healed.

Living Songs

Just as God can turn all things to his purpose, we can make of any situation a hymn of praise. Everything comes from God - even those things we tend to think of as our own; like our bodies, our breathing, our gifts and our possessions. We have come from God like sparks from an eternal fire, and we will go back to Him. All that happens in between is happening in His knowledge and under the gaze of His loving eye. If we can turn ugly moments into beautiful ones for His name's sake we can be sure of our reward. So much warrants His praise that all of heaven sings night and day, a song that will go on for all eternity. When we raise our thoughts to Him in the midst of worldly affairs, when we pause from a menial task, or invoke His name in our suffering, we too are praising, we too are living songs.

God's Presence in the World

Sometimes all we need do is take God in, the way a new-born baby takes a first breath – this too is prayer. To look in awe at a flowering cherry tree, or to stand speechless gazing up at wisps of clouds, or to walk along a stretch of golden sand at sundown - any or all of these things when done in union with God are ways of enjoying His company, His creativity, and joyful love. It's like saying 'I am open to your ways O God, I see you in all that you have made. I am aware of your presence, and I sense your power. Your fatherly protection is like a cloak around me. The vast expanses of oceans are there because you formed them, so too the trees and the countless stars. When I look at all these things in wonderment I know dear God that I am truly blessed, but it is in looking into the pained eyes of my suffering brothers and sisters in Christ that my heart can be truly opened, for they too are a showing forth of Your presence in the world.'

Adoration and the Housebound

We can draw boundaries round love. We can box ourselves in, putting limits where God puts none. Adoration can take place before a beautiful hand crafted monstrance in a sacred designated place, but we can also adore Christ, present as He is in a sick relative, or in spouse whose faculties are failing, or in the housebound. God's humility is such that although He alone is worthy of glory and honour and praise He stands to one side, makes Himself small and then urges us to bring His message and Himself to those around us. When we step out of ourselves, when we gaze with eyes of love on another human being who is suffering, we gaze on the crucified Christ. The more enduring the gaze the deeper the journey will be into the mystery of limitless love. It is there that we find Jesus. It is there that adoration takes place. He is at the centre of our lives. Without God we just would not be.

God is with us

To the man in prison, God is with us. To the woman sleeping under the railway bridge, God is with us. To the family struggling on a meagre income, God is with us. To the sick, the desperate, the lonely, God is with us.

Every pain of ours is shared by Jesus; every agony borne by the sinless one is our agony too. He knows the depth of human suffering, the anguish of desertion, the cruelty of blows. He knows the height from which souls fall; the dangers and temptations that prevail. But His message remains the same – God is with us.

The Rosary and the Cross

How comforting it is to think how a set of beads in the hands of someone ill or distressed or dying can have such healing power. Not necessarily in a direct way, for we all must die at some point, and none of us is immune from suffering, but the rosary has power to heal through the bond that it creates between us and our Mother, and through the great unity we know exists right across the world when Christians pray together.

It is the world that heals bit by bit, and we can rejoice in being partakers in such collaborative work – even in our distress and even in our dying we can be healers and bring assistance to the stranger on a far shore as well as the friend. The story of the gospel as told through the beads is our story too, and the mysteries employ us in many different ways as we imitate what they contain. We are like ships on the waves but above us always is the guiding star, we are like children running free in the fields under a watchful eye, but most of all we are heirs to a kingdom that through prayer and fidelity will one day be ours, when we are one in God.

Further into Mystery

We might ask ourselves a hundred questions about life, about why things happen, and more often than not there'll be no immediate answer. Yet sometimes we can witness acts of such extraordinary charity and compassion especially in the midst of human suffering that have the power to speak to us, not providing answers, but providing means for our enlightenment. It is as if these actions themselves are saying, 'we do not know, we are like you, we cannot understand, but we recognise a woundedness that has no voice at all, a void that invites us further into mystery, and closer to the call.'

A Single Prayer

A single prayer can melt what is frozen, the warm breath of compassion can comfort the afflicted, the beauty of God that one may be blind to, can in a moment of prayer, reveal itself in a way that convinces, compelling the heart to go forth and tell.

Awakening

'I am Easter', exclaimed the child
And as I gazed into his eyes
I journeyed to my youth
And found in welcoming spaces
Flowers like those we picked from across the brook...
Yet still I stood.

'I am Easter', said the child again
His voice sounding older than his years -
Yet not uneasy on the ear
As I journeyed to my age,
And still I stood,
Waiting to hear.

'I am Easter', said the child
And suddenly then
A pealing of bells
Across the miles that
Found me trembling at their thrill
And falling to my knees
I gazed anew on
The chaste face of a boy
Who down through centuries is come
As aspect of God's glory,
As radiance of the Son.

Hearts Ablaze

Vincentian Fire

"Justice is a fixed star which human societies try to follow from their uncertain orbits. It can be seen from different points of view, but justice itself remains unchanged."

Blessed Frederic Ozanam

Rights of Others

The parent can be no more certain than the child about the future,
A balloon held by a piece of string in a little peach of a hand
Can be whipped away by a playful gust of wind in an instant,
For life is uncertain even at its colourful best.
But the one who has climbed their own mountains in life,
And though wearied, reached summits invisible,
Can stake a claim
On the rock of lasting truths, and make a stand
With fellow combatants -
Unarmed in a military sense,
But each day taking up the fight
For the rights of others until that war is won.

"The poor are for us the sacred images of that God whom we do not see, and not knowing how to love him in any other way; we love him through the poor."

Blessed Frederic Ozanam

We reverence the faces of those we see
In place of Him whose face we cannot see.
Their streets and homes become the hallowed ground we walk upon -
When down at heel and well-shod walk as one.

"Go then; courageously advancing moment by moment along the path on which God has placed you in order to reach Him."

St Louise de Marillac

Wait, Lord, wait! I'm coming!
Though my steps falter
I'll be true to you, for where else am I to go?
Let me be mindful that you are my companion
The only power that I have
Is gifted to me by you -
Power to love others through Your action in me
And power to change
Within myself what needs changing
So as to better imitate
Your attributes and love.

"Perfection consists in a constant perseverance to acquire the virtues and become proficient in their practice, because on God's road, not to advance is to fall back since man never remains in the same condition."

St Vincent de Paul

Guide me by the hand Lord
And when I stop to admire a flower or a beautiful view
May I see always aspects of your goodness
And when I search within
Realising that this day has been like too many
Other days, energise me Lord,
Fill me with vision and grace
To move forward
To take the rough with the smooth
Thorns with roses
Knowing that in all places
And at all times
In rich and poor
You are present.
May the paths I walk be sanctified
May I find in your footsteps

A fragrance not of this world
But wafting through it
On the breath of the Spirit's love.

"You know the will of God cannot be made known more clearly in events than when they happen without our intervention or in a way other than we requested."

St Vincent de Paul

I saw God's hand in what had come about,
The sheer beauty and brilliance in the
Working of his will
Where prayer had been unuttered yet uttered still
In silent reaches of the heart, hidden and deep.
Marvelling at His work
Seeing how the sun was shining on faraway trees
I came to realise
That in terms of goodness
And grace and fatherliness
The will of God
The providence of God
The eye of the heart of Him
Is ever open and near.

"Do not be upset if things are not as you would want them to be for a long time to come. Do the little you can very peacefully and calmly so as to allow room for the guidance of God in your lives. Do not worry about the rest."

St Louise de Marillac

Neither calendar nor clock can be of use
Pointless to speculate
Or circle dates in red ink,
The world seems to be on a go-slow of late
And so I must be patient... and wait.
Perseverance is the name of the boat
And for now I opt to travel at a speed that God himself ordains -
For who can measure that?
Head bowed a little against prevailing winds
I'll keep going like one who has just set sail

Hand steady, heart set on progress,
Reliant on neither needle nor gauge.

"Let us go in simplicity where merciful Providence leads us, content to see the stone on which we should step without wanting to discover all at once and completely the windings of the road."

Blessed Frédéric Ozanam

I am crossing the stream
Finding purchase for my feet on cold stones that are steady
Though slippery with moss and algae.
Little water splashes randomly dapple their surfaces
And I can never know
Where the next one is going to show or
Whether my movement has effected it
Or if it's just water running its course.

A pilgrim soul may come ashore
In hope of new beginnings
A fresh start on ground steadier than the rougher seas they've known
With a wind-chill factored loneliness
That cuts through to the bone.

May their search for security and safety
Bring them to a new place
A home from home.

"God wants only our hearts."

St Louise de Marillac

In the most unpromising of moments
A breakthrough can emerge
And leave us in awe
Of the power and the glory
And the all-round goodness
Of the loving God
Who surprises us
And shows us over and over
That where He is, love is
And neither time
Nor doubt
Nor faith spread thinly
Can keep Him away -
All He desires is us
And that too is love -
'I am who am.'
Yearns to hear
Our voices and laughter
Our cries and our praises:
The songs and joys of His children.

"For the love of God, my dear Sister, practice great gentleness toward the poor and toward everyone. Try to satisfy as much by words as by actions. That will be very easy for you if you maintain great esteem for your neighbour: the rich because they are above you, the poor because they are your masters."

St Louise de Marillac

Smile

Sometimes a kind look is a gift in itself
As the eyes often convey what is in the soul
And like a cup that runs over
Light spills out along the road on which we travel
And others hungering or thirsting
In ice-houses of loneliness
Find solace in a human face
That gazes on their face
Even if only for an instant

For grace and its lasting effect
Can never be measured by us
Who possess only narrow ways of thinking
Grace transforms, warms, energises
And stokes fires
Lord knows we carry wealth if the truth be told
By way of temple light and candle glow.

"Peace of heart – without it, no good can make us happy. With it, every trial, even the approach of death, can be borne."

Blessed Frédéric Ozanam

I wish you peace of a thousand years
Bedded in valleys of silent snows
I wish you peace of eternal beauty
Enshrined in a rustic rambling rose
I wish you peace surpassing gifts
That greatness might impart
I wish you the gift that comes from God -
The gift of a peaceful heart.

"It is our vocation to set people's hearts ablaze, to do what the Son of God did, who came to light a fire on earth in order to set it ablaze with His love."

Blessed Fréderic Ozanam

May there be Fire

May there be fire
Licking flames
Tongues proclaiming
The glory of God's name

May there be fire
May there be gatherings
Around the flames
And hands held out in hope
May there be joy at the sight of light
And may love be a warm winter coat
On days when we need it most
May love, precious love satisfy our hunger
And strengthen the bolts on the door
So that nothing outside can harm us
And hearts ablaze can be free
To burn and tell of the story
Of the One who set all hearts free.

"Charity is the Samaritan who pours oil on the wounds of the traveller who has been attacked. But, it is justice's role to prevent the attacks."

Blessed Frédéric Ozanam

Every time we pray we start again. We sprinkle the water of words onto dry soil. We make room for new growth and use whatever tools we have at our disposal to tend the garden of the soul. And in this way we make a contribution to the order of things. We rectify, weed out, restore and trust to God that in our praying we maintain and build on our little corner of good ground - for there is good ground in many souls the world over, all of which have His name written on them , each the work of His hands.

"I felt a great attraction for the holy humanity of Our Lord and I desired to honour and imitate it insofar as I was able in the person of the poor and of all my neighbours."

St Louise de Marillac

Holy Humanity

Am I to take the stairs
And when at the turn
Where the great window admits the light,
Might I behold Him there?

Or maybe, if into the wilds I go,
Will I know His voice if I hear movement among the grasses
That all in a body seem to move
At some unheard command?

Or will it be by the sea
When I flee there from the world
That I will hear that still same voice
And I will know though no-one tells me
That it is God who speaks?

The truth is I do not know
As to where and when and how I will encounter my Lord
But let that not deter me,
But rather fill me with expectancy

That round the bend of this flowing river of minutes
that the world calls time

My Lord will present Himself
In sacred, even tattered, visible surprise

That will cause my eyes to fill with tears of gladness

Knowing beyond all doubt,
Beyond all cosmic signs,
That I am one with Him,
And life in Him is mine.

"Live simply, so that all may simply live"

St Elizabeth Ann Seton

If My Eyes Should Light Upon Your Face

Come to my assistance, Lord
If my eyes should light upon your face
Along a shadowy sweep of streets
And if my instinct should alert me to the truth
That you walk among us
Housed in the stranger
As well as in the friend.

Help me to reach out
So that my extended arm
And open heart
Will give as much as can be given;
For all is given in you.

"Be attentive to the voice of grace."

St Elizabeth Ann Seton

Lord, make me attentive to the voice of grace,
Quell any emotions that drain me of reserves
Open my ears to your wisdom
As I lean on the gate of each new day or undertaking,
Fearlessly trusting
That you're there already
Waiting for me -

Sun in the morning
Moon by night
And even then
An inner stronger light.

Index:

A Calvary of Sorts 30
A Single Prayer 126
Accomplished 96
Adoration and the Housebound 122
Advent Poem 57
And He showed them His hands and His feet.... 107
Answering 74
Ardglass Harbour 62
Arranging the Flowers 59
Autumn Poem 12
Awakening 127
Ballycastle Beach 1
Beauty and the Cross 93
Before an Icon 114
Beyond the gate 50
Cavehill, Belfast 60
Cherry Tree - North Belfast 16
City Sunset 64
Coast and Glen 6
Come, Holy Spirit 40
Crucifix 109
Curfew 23
Cushendun Beach 5
Dawn Chorus 70
Derelict House in the Glens 82
Desert 51
Divis Mountain 80
Dolphins 63
Dream for the Children of Light 58
Earth Hour Poem 19
Easter Morning, Knocknacarry 81
Ecology 43
Exaltation of the Cross 95
Fire of God 41
Followers of the Way 98

For a friend who has passed on	53
Further into Mystery	125
Gaudete Garden	56
Gazes	66
Glenariff Waterfall	61
Go Forth and Tell	45
Go to the Cross	91
God is with us	123
God's Presence in the World	121
Going Places	69
Good Friday	94
Good Friday (2)	108
Grace	55
Graves	37
Hail, O Cross, Our Only Hope	105
Healing	100
Healing Body of Christ	112
Heaven and Earth	26
Home	67
I am what I am in God	18
I shall lift my eyes to the hills (Psalm 120)	36
In the White of the Fire	76
Joy	2
Judas	34
LAUDATO SI', mi' Signore"	20
Living Songs	120
Lord of all	117
Loughareema – The Vanishing Lake	68
Lourdes – A Personal Reflection	72
Love	38
Love can make it happen	77
Mary of the Kind Eyes	87
Mercy is a River	71
Miracles of Grace	21
Muintir na Mara	32
Music	28
Nailed to the Wood	97

Nativity	46
Nativity of the Blessed Virgin Mary	25
Nature's Child	35
Noise of the world	47
Nora B	8
Northern Foreshore	4
Nothing but the skies	42
Patrick on Slemish Mountain	84
Poverty and Riches	22
Presence	48
Purpose	54
Questions and Answers	7
Rathlin Island	83
Reconciliation	14
Remembrance	85
Rosary Musings in May	86
Rose Garden	49
Scarlet Blooms	99
Setting Out	73
Sigh	116
Sight	31
Sorrowful Mysteries	101
Space for God	75
Suffering – Mary and us	113
Tantum Ergo	29
Taunting Voices	111
Temple	119
The Cherry Trees	9
The God Within	115
The Great Call	52
The Hills	39
The Master	10
The Power of God	3
The Rosary and the Cross	124
The Whole Picture	103
The Window of His Eyes	17
Tollymore Forest	79

Transformation – Lenten Poem 15
Tree of Mercy 106
Trees 33
Truest Vision 110
Two or Three 11
Until I Rest in Thee 13
Visitation 24
Water 65
Wheat 27
Willow 78
Wings 44
Within The Wounds 104
Words 118